Anxiety
Deal with it
before it ties you up in knots

Joey Mandel • Illustrated by Ted Heeley

James Lorimer & Company Ltd., Publishers
Toronto

You listen to your teacher calling out the names of kids to read aloud. **Suddenly, your heart starts beating so hard and fast** you think the other kids must be able to hear it.

Your face floods red, your eyes dart around the room. You catch the eye of the kid who is guaranteed to laugh at you and **call you stupid.** You think you are going to pass out. You sink deep into your desk, but **you can't make yourself disappear.**

You are experiencing anxiety.

Everyone worries. **Your body is hard wired to warn you** about the presence of danger and to respond to it.

Fear is not always a bad thing.

But anxiety is a fear reaction you feel when there isn't anything really very dangerous around. Instead of protecting you from real danger, your fear response starts to **interfere with your ability to cope** and to calm yourself.

In this book, you'll learn more about anxiety. You'll learn how it can snowball into meltdowns and avoidance. And you'll also **learn how to face your fears** and control the anxiety you feel.

Contents

What is Anxiety?

Anxiety is based in fear, and **everyone is afraid of something**, right? There are things it is natural to be a little afraid of:

- the unknown

- creepy crawlies

- getting hurt

- the dark

- dangerous animals

- being alone

- heights

- something bad happening to a loved one

But what if you fear things that don't seem to bother other people or that bother them just a little? What about:

- people laughing at you
- being late
- the future
- change
- failing
- rejection
- rules
- global issues

If you worry about little problems a lot or if you worry about big problems all the time, that is anxiety, and it can interfere with your daily living and enjoyment of life.

Anxiety 101

Everyone is at the party.

Anxiety can affect your...

Sasha is nervous about the math test.

Hey, Sasha, can I borrow a pencil?

Morgan is worried that her bff is angry with her.

She had no right to say that to me.

Come on, Marco! Pack faster or you'll be late for camp.

Anxiety 101

Anxiety or Survival Instinct?

Why do people act the way they do? Survival instinct can make us act in aggressive or passive ways in the face of danger or a challenge. But sometimes weird behaviour is a response to inner feelings of stress. Read the following scenarios and decide if the reaction shows Anxiety or Survival Instinct.

Read-aloud Reaction

1 Rowan has to read out loud in front of a group of cool kids. His palms are sweaty and he feels nauseated. He yells at the kid beside him that she is making too much noise with her papers.

Anxiety.
These are typical physical responses to stress. However, since it is beginning to impact his behaviour and the way he talks to others, it shows signs of anxiety.

The Big Jump

2 Jamie goes diving with her dad off of a huge cliff. Her heart is pounding so loud she can hear it in her head.

Survival Instinct.
This is a natural physical response to a scary adventure.

3 Lunch Number Crunch

As a special treat, Ivan goes out for lunch with his friends. He realizes that it is going to cost more than he thought. He calculates his order and the tip in his head over and over during the meal.

Anxiety.
Money is a normal thing to worry about, but what makes this more than worry and more similar to anxiety is the repetitive thinking.

4 Historical Heartbeat

Sophie has a history presentation to do in front of her class. Her heart is beating really fast, but she is telling jokes with her friends as she waits her turn.

Survival Instinct.
Sophie has a presentation to do in front of her class and her heart is beating really fast but she is telling jokes with her friends as she waits her turn.

5 April Fool

On April 1, the teacher zombie-walks into the class with bloody makeup all over her face. Leon screams, but then sits down and laughs.

Survival Instinct.
This is a typical response to something scary, but once the threat disappears, Leon is able to continue with his day. Therefore, it is not anxiety.

6 Knock 'Em Dead-line

Keshia's social studies group is going to miss a deadline. Keshia orders the others to reorganize their assignments and yells at the teacher that they need more time. She says over and over that they will not be done in time.

Anxiety
In some cases, a little pressure helps students focus, but in this case, the pressure or stress is overwhelming her and preventing her from completing her tasks.

7 Missing Persons

Zack's friends are not at their usual table — or in the cafeteria at all. Zack feels tension in his shoulders and feels off balance. He walks over to another table and sits down with another group of kids.

Survival Instinct
This is not an example of anxiety. Zack has some physical feelings of nervousness to a slightly stressful situation, and then finds a solution to his problem.

8 Best Friends For Fighting

Daisy has a disagreement with her friend, but they talk it out. When Daisy gets home, she bursts into tears. She repeats the story to her mom, her dad, her brother, and four friends on the phone.

Anxiety.
These behaviours are possible signs of social anxiety. Daisy is not able to move on and stop thinking about a situation that has been resolved.

9 Squeeze Them Tight

Sandro hates being away from his parents. Each time his parents go out together at night, he worries that he will never see them again. He begs them not to go out with their friends.

Anxiety.
Sandro thinks about these worries a lot and asks other people to stop doing things they want to do for fear of what might happen.

10 Test Pattern

Zoe has a test next week. She lies in bed every night planning when she will study and thinking about her notes.

Anxiety.
Thinking about notes and studying is effective, if it helps you take action. However, if planning and thinking are based in worry and keep a person up at night, it is not productive.

Dear Anxiety Counsellor

Q: I am ten years old. I don't know why, but when I am told that it is time to go to an activity, like baseball or chess club, my whole body tenses up. It is not like I am afraid of going outside or being part of a group, but at the words "It's time to go," my heart beats like thunder. I freak out and run up to my room. My mom points out that I like the activity once I am there. I have fun and get along with the other kids. I am always happy that I went, but the next week I have the same feeling of dread when I am told I have to leave home. Should I just stay home until I feel better about going out?

— **Homebody**

A: Fear builds through avoidance. If each time you keep giving in to your fear of leaving the house, it will become harder and harder to face your fear. Each time you stay home and feel safe and relaxed at home, your brain thinks you feel that way because you stayed inside and did not go out. This becomes a cycle and it will become harder and harder to go outside. But if you go out and face your fear, you realize that you can have fun, and you overcome your fear. Your body might experience the stress, but your mind reassures you that you can face the stress and survive it. It does get easier each time.

Q: I'm terrified of bees and wasps. When I see a bee, I feel like screaming and running away. I *want* to walk calmly to the other side of the street or just walk away, but I can't. I'm paralyzed with fear, even if I know the bee probably won't hurt me. What's going on?

— **Buzzing Off**

A: Your body is designed to react to dangerous things to protect you — it's called Fight, Flight, or Freeze. When your eyes see something that might injure you, your "feeling" brain sends warning messages throughout your body. Your "thinking" brain recognizes possible danger and decides to face the danger (Fight), run away (Flight), or stay still until the danger is past (Freeze). When you see a bee, your feeling brain reacts so strongly that it shuts off messages from your thinking brain. Your thinking brain might be trying to tell you to slow down, breathe, and walk back slowly, but those messages are not getting through because your feeling brain is shutting down your usual problem-solving skills.

Q: I have always been a worrier. I worry about something bad happening to me or to someone I love. I often imagine my parents getting divorced. I worry about failing and being laughed at. I worry about not being able to go to university someday, and then not getting a job when I am older. Lately, my worrying has been getting out of control. The pain and tightness in my chest happen if I think someone looks at me in an off way, when a teacher calls my name, or when I need to leave the house. I am not sleeping well because the sheets irritate my skin and my body feels like there are fireworks inside. Why can I control my anxiety sometimes but not others?

— **Sleepless in Stressville**

A: If you are an anxious person, sometimes you will be able to manage your worries and have control over them. But sometimes, you won't. It's good that you see that you are having more stress than normal. The trick is to figure out why. Is there a major event happening in your life? Are there extra pressures on you? Have you changed your diet or stopped exercising? You might need to slow down a little and take time to smell the roses — actually breathing in deeply and exhaling slowly can calm you down and make it easier to think clearly about the sources of your anxiety.

Q: I can't stand presenting on stage. During a school performance, I'm so nervous I can't see in front of me. So sometimes I actually trip, and people laugh. When it's time for me to say something, I feel like I can't hear or think, so no words come out of my mouth. When I am done, I feel really stupid and someone in the class always makes a joke about how dumb I am. We have a school play coming up and my parents and teachers want me to be in it. They keep telling me that I need to face my fears, but how is making a fool of myself going to help me?

— **Stage Fright**

A: Your teachers and parents have it half right: You do need to face your fears. If you avoid ever speaking in public, your fear will only grow. But I think you need to talk with them and let them know that you need more support. Having to do a play in front of the whole school is probably too much for you. That is not gradually facing your fear; that is jumping into the deep end when you know you can't swim. Getting over your fear will involve gradually facing smaller fears in a situation where you can succeed. See if you can start with a performance just in front of your friends and family. Then try a part that has you only on stage for a short time when most of the attention is on someone else. Then you won't risk actually breaking a leg!

Myths

Anxiety is all in your head.

The fast beating of your heart, sweating, and nausea you feel are all real.

Anxiety is your body's real response to a danger message from something your brain notices in your environment.

Avoid things that make you anxious.

When you escape whatever makes you anxious, you feel safe. Your brain equates feeling safe with getting away from your fear, so your fear of that thing grows.

Feeling fear is the only sign of anxiety.

Anxiety is not just being afraid of scary things. Anxiety can be going over and over thoughts in your head, or reactions like tantrums to avoid situations.

DID YOU KNOW?

• Anxiety is more common in girls than in boys.

Dive right into your fears.

Anxiety can grow if you try to face fears that are just too scary and too hard. Exposure to what you fear can be too overwhelming, and your brain only remembers how horrible it felt.

Anxious people are weak.

Every day, anxious people do things that make them feel nervous and afraid. That's not weak!

There is no cure for anxiety.

Anxiety can be treated with therapy. Talk about fears and find solutions. Some children and adults see their doctors about medication that will help them feel less stressed.

- Anxiety is the most common mental health issue among children and youth.

- Anxiety affects 6.5% of young people.
- Anxiety can be confused with anger and depression.

Does it seem like you're always afraid?

You are worried, but don't know why. You spend sleepless nights thinking about all the bad things that will happen. You feel nausea almost every day.

Your heart beats viciously when you even hear the word for what you fear. Your whole body tells you to run away when you have to confront it.

Do you suffer from anxiety?

DEAR DR. SHRINK-WRAPPED...

Q: Sometimes I have a hard time with decisions. For example, last week I got super pumped about going to a basketball game, but my friends planned a party for the same day. I decided to go to the game, but the whole time I was there, I wished I was at the party. I couldn't stop thinking about what the other kids were doing. I kept rethinking my choice in my head. It made me feel sick to my stomach and I came home upset. So I missed the party and I ruined the basketball game for myself. My parents tell me that this is anxiety, but I am not afraid of anything.

— *Fearless Fretter*

A: We often associate anxiety with big fears or specific phobias. But Dr. Shrink-Wrapped is here to tell you that anxiety is a lot more than that. Your parents are onto the fact that you have a hard time enjoying the moment because of uncontrollable thoughts about what you are missing. Anxiety can be the kind of repetitive thinking you experience when you wonder if you made the right decision. The continuous mental worry is causing your body to react in a physical way, by feeling sick to your stomach. Think about this, Fretter: Every decision can be a good one if you make the most of the situation while you are in it. And the good news is that knowing you have anxiety is the first step to overcoming it. Read on!

Q: It drives me crazy when my teacher rearranges our class. Without notice, I come in and my desk has been moved to another place in the room. Some kids get excited and look around to find out where they will be sitting. When I can't find my desk where I left it, my body freezes up. I felt safe sitting in my desk and so I feel lost when it is moved. Everyone from my parents to my classmates says that I need to get over it. I respect the fact that some people see moving desks as a game. Why can't people respect that I see it as a problem?

— *Safe-Seat Student*

A: Safe, you're right, everyone has different things that bother them and people need to be respectful of that. You could tell other students that it does not help you when they dismiss your feelings and simply tell you to get over them. But trust Dr. Shrink-Wrapped: It's more important that you get your parents and teacher to understand the challenge this is for you. If you share some insight about how you feel about knowing your desk is in one place, they can be more sympathetic to your feelings of anxiety. Even though most people would not consider this a problem, you do. And it's as serious to you as other issues are to other people. If you let them know that this is your challenge and it is something that you are working to overcome, they might be less dismissive of it.

QUIZ

Worrywart or cool as a cucumber?

Take this quiz to find out if you let anxiety get the better of you. How many of these statements are true about you?

1. I freak out over lots of things.

2. When something makes me uncomfortable, I freeze on the spot.

3. It's important to create schedules and rules to set order.

4. If something bothers me, I run away.

5. I'm always talking to myself inside my head to calm myself down.

6. I always need to go back and check that I've done something correctly.

7. Having everything the same is very important.

8. When I'm stressed, my chest gets tight and achy.

9. I sweat when I'm not hot or physically active.

10. I often feel helpless to deal with situations.

11. I don't go places where I don't feel in control.

12. I have one best friend and don't hang with anyone else.

13. I feel relaxed and in control when I am alone with my favourite things.

14. When I do or say something I regret, I repeat the scenario over and over in my head.

15. When I say goodbye to people, sometimes I think that it will be the last time I ever see them.

16 Reassurance from my family and friends is important to me.

17 I focus on and remember the negatives in a situation.

18 When I think about what will happen, I often imagine a terrible outcome.

19 I think that other people are always talking and thinking about me.

20 I get very upset if I forget something that I need for school or an activity.

Did you get a lot of TRUEs?
Maybe it's time to take a look at **how anxiety is affecting your life,** and **talk to** someone about **ways to cope with it.**

Keeping Track

Once you understand what stresses you and the way you feel, you can do a lot to decrease your anxiety and cope with stressful situations. It's important to track the following:

The Good

Start tracking positive situations. Think about and remember the environments, activities, and times that make you feel calm, confident, and relaxed. Take note of the situations in which you are productive and capable.

The Bad

Keep track of negative situations. Note the places, activities, and times that make you feel anxious. Write down where you are, who you are with, and what the people around you are doing. Are they talking to you, asking you a lot of questions, or placing demands on you?

What You Feel

Track your physical feelings, like a sore stomach or trouble breathing, as well as your emotional state or your mood. Try to examine your own anxiety in more detail. Once you are stressed, and your body reacts to the stress, do you feel nervous and worried, sad, or angry?

What You Do

When you become stressed, how do you act? Do you try to avoid the cause of your anxiety? Do you eat junk food? Do you yell or punch someone? Do you keep rethinking the situation? Do you have rituals that you complete over and over to try to bring order to your life?

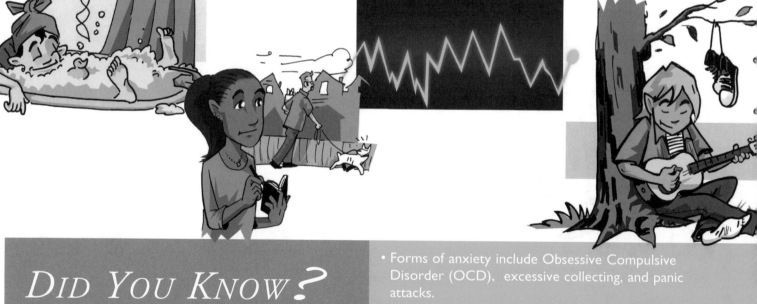

DID YOU KNOW?

• Forms of anxiety include Obsessive Compulsive Disorder (OCD), excessive collecting, and panic attacks.

What You Think

Once things become hard, what do you say to yourself? Is your inner voice an excited, energetic cheerleader, whispering positive messages in your ear? "Go, Go, Go! You can do it! I know you can!" Or are you your worst enemy? Do you tell yourself how hopeless it is? and that there is no way that you can succeed? "Give up now. It is too hard for you."

✓ Do realize that many other children feel nervous, worried, scared, unsure, and anxious too.

✓ Do realize the people who love and support you can also be the people who increase your anxiety.

✓ Do know that you can overcome your fear.

✓ Do understand that the more you think excessively about your fear, explain it to everyone, get sympathy for it, and avoid it, the more your fear grows.

✓ Do encourage yourself and use a positive inner voice.

✓ Do limit your inner voice by allowing yourself to think through things once.

✓ Do tell yourself that just because something bad happened once, it might not happen again.

✓ Do think about all the possible outcomes and tell yourself not to focus on the worst ones.

✗ Don't think that you are powerless to overcome your fear.

✗ Don't think that nobody else has fears, worries, panics, or dreads.

✗ Don't think that you can solve your stress by running away.

✗ Don't let yourself repeatedly rethink the situation.

✗ Don't ignore positive outcomes.

✗ Don't assume that because something bad happened once, it is bound to happen again.

✗ Don't always think about the worst outcomes.

- People with OCD do certain things over and over to try to calm their inner stress.
- Excessive collecting comes from a person's need to control and set order to a part of his or her world.

- A panic attack can cause sweating, pounding heart, trembling, nausea, shortness of breath, chest pain, and strong negative feelings.

The **Peace seeker**

You got almost no work done in class: you were too busy going nuts because of the kid sitting next to you. Yes, he kept breathing deeply and it did make a lot of noise. But did it help when you hit your desk with your hands, rolled your eyes, and yelled for the teacher?

He does annoy you.

His behaviour is **totally uncool.** But think about this: **Does telling him how disruptive he is change his behaviour?**

X Don't forget that everyone has challenges in life.

X Don't think you know what is going on inside someone else's brain and body.

✓ Do try to think about your own behaviour instead of that of others.

✓ Do understand that whatever someone else is doing might be helping him or her cope with a huge challenge.

✓ Do understand that anxiety is hardest on the person who has it.

X Don't think that people choose to be anxious.

X Don't get caught up in being upset by someone else's behaviour.

✓ Do understand that someone's repetitive questions might be to calm and reassure inner worries.

✓ Do understand that someone's controlling behaviour might be caused by feeling out of control on the inside.

✓ Do consider whether your anxiety is making you react to other people's behaviour.

✓ Do distract yourself and move on to thinking about something else.

✓ Do take ten slow, deep breaths when the behaviour of others bothers you.

X Don't get so focused on what someone else is doing that you cause yourself stress.

X Don't be uncaring of the experiences of others.

X Don't use put-downs or insults when someone's behaviour is bothering you.

X Don't rush in to deal with someone else's problem.

21

QUIZ

How do you react when someone is experiencing anxiety?

Do you ignore it? Run away? Get angry or frustrated? Try to help? There are three standard reactions that people have when someone around them is anxious: Avoid, Attack, or Assist. You might Avoid or Attack because the other person's behaviour is raising your own anxiety level. But if you try to understand what triggers other people's anxieties and help them calm down, it can calm you down. Take this quiz and then check out your behaviour on the next page.

Cruel School

There is a girl who has been in the same class as you since kindergarten. She hates coming to school. She used to scream and cry in the halls and make a huge scene every morning. Now she no longer has meltdowns. She just acts weird. She comes late every day, and spends the school day with her body slouched over, her head down, and her hair in her face. What do you do?
a) Tell her to get over it.
b) Ignore her. Clearly she doesn't want the attention.
c) Ask her if she is feeling okay.

FTW

You are playing video games with your friend and you are winning. As the game goes on, she gets more and more upset. She starts snapping at you and cheating at the game. Do you:
a) Say you are hungry and would like to take a break from the game?
b) Snap back at her and call her a cheater?
c) Start losing on purpose so she can catch up?

Take-Charge Type

You have been put into groups for a project. One of your group members just takes over. He insists he knows the only way to get an A+ on the assignment. He picks the topic, assigns everyone roles, and won't stop talking. He will not listen to the ideas of anyone in the group. How do you react?
a) Say nothing and let him lead the group. Maybe he knows what he's talking about.
b) Politely and clearly state that other members of the group might have ideas and would like a chance to share them.
c) Tell him he is being controlling and to stop bossing everyone around.

Very Scary

You love horror movies, but your friend hates them. She says they totally freak her out and give her nightmares. What should you do?
a) Stop watching scary movies and always go with her movie choice.
b) Tell her she's a wimp and make her watch all your favourite horror movies with you. She's got to learn to get over her fears.
c) Suggest some action movies with a little suspense in them.

Test of Nerves

The teacher announces that there are five more minutes to write the test. The student sitting next to you gets really upset. He keeps repeating that he will not have time to finish and that he needs more time. What do you do?
a) Tell him that he is being too loud and that you can't concentrate.
b) Plug your ears and keep reviewing your test.
c) Tell him to take some deep breaths and to try to use the five minutes as well as he can.

Father Figure

Your dad totally stresses you out. He's a great guy and really loves you, but he is intense and over-controlling. He is always worrying about you and trying to manage every little part of your life. Do you
a) Take a deep breath and find a time to talk with him about how his worrying makes you feel?
b) Tell him that he is annoying you and to leave you alone?
c) Ignore him and give him short answers with as little information as possible?

Presentation Problems

Your friend gives a presentation in front of the class and it is terrible. She forgets half her lines and stutters. You can see from the back of the room how much she is sweating and shaking. What do you do?
a) Tell her she was amazing and that there were no problems at all.
b) Praise her on the strength of her research and then give her one suggestion for next time.
c) Tell her she should never do presentations again.

Whirl Wind

Your little brother is scared of the wind. Every time he goes outside, he screams and cries and clings to your mom's leg. What do you do?
a) Tell your mom to stop babying him. Some tough love is needed here.
b) Ask your mom's advice about how you should act when your brother is scared.
c) When it's windy, offer your brother extra hugs and kisses and buy him a treat.

Exam Exception

Your friend is super smart and does well in all her classes, but she gets stressed around exam time. She studies really hard but always bombs her exams. Do you:
a) Make fun of her and tell her not to bother studying 'cause she is going to tank anyway?
b) Tell her not to worry because she is so smart and will be fine?
c) Encourage her to talk to the teacher and explain about her anxiety around tests?

Going Downhill

Your brother seemed excited to go skiing with the family, but when he gets to the top of the hill, he freezes and makes a big scene. He refuses to go down the hill and keeps you all waiting for forty-five minutes. What do you do?
a) Wait quietly by the side, saying nothing, or skiing away on your own (with permission).
b) Tell your brother to find a spot to focus on and ski just to that point. Ski with him and stop at the point you decided on together.
c) Tell your parents to leave him at the top of the hill and keep skiing. He'll come down when he gets cold enough.

Answers	b) Assist	6. a) Assist	c) Avoid
1. a) Attack	c) Attack	b) Attack	9. a) Attack
b) Avoid	4. a) Avoid	c) Avoid	b) Avoid
c) Assist	b) Attack	7. a) Avoid	c) Assist
2. a) Assist	c) Assist	b) Assist	10. a) Avoid
b) Attack	5. a) Attack	c) Attack	b) Assist
c) Avoid	b) Avoid	8. a) Attack	c) Attack
3. a) Avoid	c) Assist	b) Assist	

Learn ways to calm your body and your mind.

If you are bothered by all kinds of things and by other people, **it will make your life harder.** If you keep focusing on things other people do that bother you, you will end up losing out on your own work and happiness. **If you can calm your body, it will help you calm your mind.**

Progressive Muscle Relaxation

This exercise tenses and relaxes different muscle groups in your body.

Open eyes wide/close eyes tightly

Point toes/flex toes

Tighten body/relax body

Open mouth/shut mouth

Scrunch cheeks/relax cheeks

Brain and Body Connection

Now link what you feel to your mind. Take off your shoes and plant the soles of your feet on the ground. Push the energy from your body into the ground. Think about something that makes you feel anxious: Picture the situation, where you are, what it looks like, who is there, and what they are saying. Think about your body and how your body is feeling.

Breathe in and out slowly, counting to five. Do it again, more slowly this time. Raise your arms high into the air and come off of your feet, onto your toes. Try to touch the sky. Come back down and continue to take deep, long breaths.

Think about something that makes you feel safe. Picture where you are, what you are doing. Focus on every sight, sound, and feeling. Push your feet back into the ground. Continue to take deep breaths, expanding your lungs.

DID YOU KNOW?

- Anxiety and depression occur together 50–60% of the time.

- Kids with anxiety can have difficulties with tasks that ne concentration and organizati

When a Meltdown Is Involved

When fear or stress is overwhelming, people with anxiety want to escape the situation. They might learn over time that having a meltdown is the only way to escape.

The meltdown cycle is a pattern that gets rid of the anxiety you feel. People around you aren't listening: they keep making you do things or stay in situations where you feel anxious. That trapped feeling grows until you finally lose control and freak out: screaming, crying, yelling, and hitting. Suddenly, everyone rushes in to calm you down and protect you from whatever is causing your huge reaction. What have you learned? Having a meltdown means you don't have to experience any more anxiety, leaving you feeling calm and safe.

But melting down to avoid problems is a bad cycle. It's only a temporary solution to your anxiety. And each time you escape your fear without facing it, it grows bigger.

There are alternatives to using meltdowns:
- Explain your fear to the people around you.
- Let people know that they haven't been listening to what you are saying you need.
- Point out that having a meltdown gets people to listen.
- Discuss your anxiety and problem-solve outside of the stressful situation.
- Show people that you are ready to try a new approach.

- Create a plan to gradually and successfully expose yourself to whatever stresses you.
- Let your support group help you follow the plan.

If you are faced with someone having a meltdown:
- Stop talking. Listen to the person having the meltdown.
- Do not try to solve the person's problem.
- Do not try to debate or reason logically with the person.
- Focus on your own slow breathing in order to keep yourself calm.
- Monitor your own body language. (Make sure you do not look angry.)
- Assess the situation. Can you figure out what triggered the meltdown? Is the trigger is still making the person anxious?
- Encourage the person to breathe.
- Talk about something funny, cute, relaxing, or happy.
- Make sure that the person is calm before you consider trying to solve the problem.

The meltdown cycle is not easy to break. Avoiding a meltdown does not mean:
- Running away from your fears.
- Getting people to give you whatever you want so that you are always relaxed.

Instead, to avoid a meltdown, you need to:
- Stop, pause, and calm yourself. Decrease your stress level so that you are able to use strategies to face your trigger.

- Anxiety is often confused with behavioural challenges or ADHD.
- 70% of cases of anxiety and other mental health issues begin during childhood.

- Only 20% of young people with anxiety and mental health challenges receive help.
- Early intervention can help decrease anxiety.

The **Witness**

Were you ever around when someone had a panic attack or a meltdown?

Do you have a friend or family member who has acted out when feeling overwhelmed with stress?

Think about what you did in those situations.

Maybe you mentioned the difficulty the person was having to someone who could help. You could have stepped in yourself to try to help calm the person down. Maybe you did nothing at all.

You have a choice when it comes to dealing with people with anxiety.

Part of the Problem

Sometimes people trying to help can make things worse:

- Witnesses might judge a person with anxiety, increasing the stress the person feels about what people think of him or her.
- Families can overprotect and shelter people with anxiety, never letting them face their fears.
- Friends and other people who care might push a person with anxiety into stressful situations, simply increasing the person's fear and feelings of lack of control.
- People might accept any behaviours and avoidance as anxiety-based and beyond a person's control.
- Anything you do that increases a person's anxiety or doesn't help them deal successfully with stress makes you part of the problem.

Part of the Solution

Life is pretty stressful for everyone. You and your parents, teachers, and friends all juggle a lot of things each day. Anyone can get caught up in the fast pace and the pressure, putting stress on themselves and others. But you have the power to lessen the anxiety everyone feels, including your own.

- Try to understand what other people might be going through.
- Realize that people can be anxious about things that don't bother you.
- Don't judge people as weak or mean when their behaviour is caused by fear or nervousness.
- Understand that any time a person successfully faces a fear, it is a step toward being less anxious.
- Take the pressure off yourself and your friends. Whether you want to deal with your own anxiety or help others deal with their stresses, it is in your power to help create safer and healthier environments and relationships.

dos and don'ts

✓ Do help slow down the pace of your life and the lives of those around you.

✓ Do realize if you are putting pressure on someone.

✓ Do try having water or juice instead of caffeinated drinks.

✓ Do try to eat as little sugar as you can.

✓ Do try to suggest bringing yoga and non-competitive exercise groups to your school.

✓ Do consider joining or starting a health and wellness club at your school.

✓ Do promote messages of slowing down and enjoying the moment.

✓ Do consider being a voice for others if you see that they are overwhelmed and can't cope.

✗ Don't think that you need to be the best at everything.

✗ Don't judge people or pressure them to be perfect.

✗ Don't point out things people have done wrong or they have forgotten to do.

✗ Don't add pressure to your life or those of the people around you.

✗ Don't use too much reason or logic when someone is upset.

✗ Don't let anxiety become someone's identity.

✗ Don't talk too much.

✗ Don't think other people's fears or worries are insignificant or unjustified.

The **Witness**

QUIZ

Do you really get it?

Okay, so you think you understand anxiety, what people worry about, and how it makes them behave. But do you really get your own response to anxiety? What would you do in the following situations? This quiz has no right or wrong answers, because each situation — and every person — is unique. Your answers may be different from the ones suggested here, but they could be right, under the circumstances.

① IN THE LOOP

Normally your friend Shaylene is fun, kind, and creative, but you are having a hard time dealing with her. She got into a serious fight with her parents, but she does not stop talking about it. She thinks she is right, and so do you, but you keep having the same conversation over and over and over. What should you do?

a) Tell her she is right and her parents are wrong.

b) Be a good friend and continue to listen.

c) Support her, but point out that she has spent a lot of time thinking and talking about the same thing.

d) Ask her if she thinks it's time to find a way to put it behind her.

e) Ask her if she would like you to help explain to her parents how much it is upsetting her.

② PANIC IN THE STREETS

You and your friends are walking home from school, and you see a kid from school sitting at the bus stop. Her eyes are wide open and she is grabbing her throat. It looks like she is gasping for air. She is sweating and shaking. She is clearly having a panic attack. What can you do?

a) Keep walking. Getting involved might make things worse.

b) Go and tell an adult you know and trust.

c) Approach the situation slowly. Look around and assess the area. Is she safe where she is? Try to ensure that people are giving her space and not crowding her.

3 SKIPPING SCHOOL

Your younger brother tells you that he hates school and never wants to go back. Do you:

a) Leave him alone?

b) Watch for the next few days and observe how he acts going to school and what happens when he gets there?

c) Let him know that most kids feel that way and try to make a list of the good things about school?

d) Sit down with him and try to figure out if there is a something new going on and if you can problem-solve it together?

5 RECESS WRECKER

Every recess, Karl follows you and your friends around. He is awkward and wrecks whatever you are playing by asking a whole bunch of questions. Lately he has been saying that he has social anxiety, that he gets nervous around people and this is how he copes with it. But Karl's way of coping with it is ruining recess for the rest of you. What do you do?

a) Pretend he isn't there and keep playing.

b) Ignore his questions but keep playing with him.

c) Tell him what he is doing well and praise his ideas when he contributes to the game.

d) Talk with a teacher about setting up a play group for him to help him gain some social skills that he needs to make him feel more confident.

4 Lunch Bunch

Your friend Emma has been getting upset with your group lately. She keeps saying that no one likes her and that she is being excluded. Today she came late to the cafeteria and got mad because you were all sitting together without her. She started going on and on about how all her so-called friends are meeting and talking about her behind her back. What should you do?

a) Ignore her complaints and focus on something fun.

b) Get her a chair and ask her what she wants to talk about.

c) Try to reassure her and point out the positives in your friendship.

d) Find a time to talk with her in private and tell her that you think she is misreading situations.

Continues . . .

6 Sister Re-Act

Your older sister has always been nice and had time for you. But lately she is in a bad mood. She wants to get into a great school, so she is under a lot of pressure. She comes home late every night because of her volunteer work and activities. Anytime you try to talk to her, she snaps at you and starts yelling that you just don't understand how important it is for her to do well. What can you do?

a) Ignore her and walk away. This is a temporary situation that has nothing to do with you.

b) Calmly say that you know that she is under stress, but that she should not take it out on you.

c) Talk with your parents about fun and easy ways to help her create a better balance in her life.

7 ROCK BAND

You and a bunch of your friends are throwing rocks into a creek behind your school. A boy in another grade sees you and starts yelling at you that throwing rocks is dangerous. He is talking really loud and repeating himself. Do you:

a) Ignore him?

b) Ask him if you can throw one more rock without him getting upset?

c) Stop throwing the rocks right away?

d) Get an adult you know and trust to help you handle the situation?

8 Twenty Questions

Your classmate Alisha keeps asking your teacher if she is doing a good job and if she is on the right track. The teacher keeps snapping that Alisha has to stop asking questions and focus on her work. But it only makes Alisha ask more questions. What can you do?

a) Accept that the situation has nothing to do with you.

b) Tell Alisha she should not bother the teacher so much.

c) Tell Alisha that she should assume that she is doing things right unless someone tells her otherwise.

d) Give Alisha encouragement and let her know she is doing a great job.

9 OH, BROTHER

Your older brother can't handle any kind of change. He needs specific rules and schedules, and your parents support him by following them consistently. You are getting tired of how his fears control the whole family, and he doesn't seem to be getting better about change. Should you:

a) Get angry and tell your parents that they need to stop treating your brother like a baby?

b) Support your family by understanding your brother's needs and following them as best you can?

c) Explain to your parents that putting your brother's needs above yours is not good for you or for him?

10 HOME, SWEET HOME

Your friend Fazi will not come to your house. When you do things together after school or on the weekend, it is always at his home. Do you:

a) Start spending more time with your other friends?

b) Keep getting together with Fazi only at his place?

c) Plan to have a few friends over and invite Fazi to come too?

d) Tell Fazi that it would mean a lot to you to have him over to your place?

e) Ask Fazi what you can do to make it easier for him to get together with you somewhere other than his place?

More Help

Help lines and Organizations

Kids Help Phone (Canada): 1-800-668-6868
Youth Crisis Hotline (USA): 1-800-448-4663
Mental Health Help line: 1-866-531-2600

Web sites

Health Canada — Just for You (youth): http://hc-sc.gc.ca/hl-vs/jfy-spv/
   youth-jeunes-eng.php
Kids Help Phone: http://www.kidshelpphone.ca
America Academy of Child and Adolescent Psychiatry Youth
   Resources: http://www.aacap.org/AACAP/Families_and_Youth/
   Youth_Resources/Home.aspx?hkey=58aaf61e-36ea-4a84-9a4c-
   58b2a434c869
Centre for Addiction and Mental Health, Anxiety Disorders: http://
   www.camh.ca/en/hospital/health_information/a_z_mental_health_and_
   addiction_information/anxiety_disorders/Pages/Anxiety_Disorders.aspx
Children's Mental Health Ontario: http://www.kidsmentalhealth.ca/
   documents/res-building-a-better-school-environment-for-youth-with-
   mental-health-and-addiction-issuesv2.pdf
Mind Your Mind: Mental Illnesses: http://www.mindyourmind.ca/
   illnesses

Books

28 Tricks for a Fearless Grade 6 by Catherine Austen. Lorimer, 2014.
A "5" Could Make Me Lose Control by Kari Dunn Buron. Autism
   Spectrum Publishing Co, 2007.
Being Me with OCD: How I Learned to Obsess Less and Live My Life by
   Alison Dotson. Free Spirit Publishing, 2014
The Complete Idiot's Guide to Controlling Anxiety by Joni E. Johnston Psy.D.
   Penguin Group, 2006.
Drawing Together to Learn about Feelings by Marge Eaton Heegaard.
   Fairview Press, 2003.
Fear This Book: Your Guide to Fright, Horror, & Things That Go Bump in the
   Night by Jeff Szpirglas. Maple Tree Press, 2006.
Minnie is Worried by Victoria Birkett. Envision communication LTD.,
   2012.
Nobody's Perfect: A Story for Children About Perfectionism by Ellen Flanagan
   Burns. Magination Press, 2008.
The Relaxation and Stress Reduction Workbook for Kids: Help for Children
   to Cope with Stress, Anxiety, and Transitions by Lawrence
   Shapiro and Robin Sprague. Instant Help Books, 2009.
The Unlikely Hero of Room 13B by Teresa Toten. Doubleday Canada,
   2013.
What to Do When Good Enough Isn't Good Enough: The Real Deal on
   Perfectionism: A Guide for Kids by Thomas S. Greenspon Ph.D. Free
   Spirit Publishing, 2014.
What to Do When You Worry Too Much: A Kid's Guide to Overcoming
   Anxiety (What to Do Guides for Kids) by Bonnie Matthews.
   Magination Press, 2006.
When No One Is Watching by Eileen Spinelli. Eerdmans Books for Young
   Readers, 2013.
Whimsy's Heavy Things by Julie Kraulis. Tundra Books, 2013.

Copyright © 2014 by Joey Mandel
Illustrations copyright © James Lorimer & Company
Ltd., Publishers
First published in the United States in 2015.

James Lorimer & Company Ltd., Publishers
acknowledges the support of the Ontario Arts
Council. We acknowledge the financial support of the
Government of Canada through the Canada Book
Fund for our publishing activities. We acknowledge the
support of the Canada Council for the Arts which last
year invested $24.3 million in writing and publishing
throughout Canada. We acknowledge the Government
of Ontario through the Ontario Media Development
Corporation's Ontario Book Initiative.

Canada   Canada Council   Conseil des Arts   ONTARIO ARTS COUNCIL
           for the Arts   du Canada   CONSEIL DES ARTS DE L'ONTARIO

Series Design: Blair Kerrigan/Glyphics

Library and Archives Canada Cataloguing in Publication

Mandel, Joey, author
        Anxiety : deal with it before it ties you up in
knots
/ Joey Mandel ; illustrated by Ted Heeley.

(Deal with it)
Includes bibliographical references.
ISBN 978-1-4594-0710-7 (bound).--ISBN 978-1-4594-
0709-1 (pbk.)

        1. Anxiety in children--Juvenile literature. I.
Heeley, Ted,
1964-, illustrator II. Title. III. Series: Deal with it
(Toronto, Ont.)

BF723.A5M35 2014   j152.4'6   C2014-903017-7

James Lorimer & Company Ltd., Publishers
317 Adelaide Street West, Suite 1002
Toronto, ON, Canada
M5V 1P9
www.lorimer.ca

Distributed in the United States by:
Orca Book Publishers
P.O. Box 468
Custer, WA, USA
98240-0468

Printed and bound in Canada.
Manufactured by Friesens Corporation in Altona,
Manitoba, Canada in August 2014.
Job #205960